SCIENCE

OUTRUNNING BULLETS

SUPERMAN™ AND THE SCIENCE OF SPEED

BY *TAMMY ENZ*

SUPERMAN CREATED BY
JERRY SIEGEL
AND **JOE SHUSTER**
BY SPECIAL ARRANGEMENT
WITH THE JERRY SIEGEL FAMILY

Published by Curious Fox, an imprint of Capstone Global Library Limited, 7 Pilgrim Street, London, EC4V 6LB – Registered company number: 6695582

www.curious-fox.com

Edited by Christopher Harbo
Designed by Bob Lentz
Production by Tori Abraham
Picture research by Eric Gohl
Originated by Capstone Global Library Limited
Printed and bound in China

ISBN 978 1 78202 498 9
20 19 18 17 16
10 9 8 7 6 5 4 3 2 1

British Library Cataloguing in Publication Data
A full catalogue record for this book is available from the British Library

Awknowledgements
Dreamstime: Chrisstanley, 9; DVIDS: NASA, 11, 26; NASA: 15 (all), 17 (bottom), 27, 28, 29, Bill Ingalls, 17 (top), DFRC/X-43A Development Team, 13; Shutterstock: Andre Coetzer, 21, Aphelleon, 7 (top), Artyom Anikeev, 19 (bottom), ChameleonsEye, 8, Digital Storm, 19 (top), Fotokostic, 7 (bottom), Gui Jun Peng, cover, Janossy Gergely, 20 (bottom), Jochen Kost, 14, Jonathan C Photography, 20 (top), Kaliva, 25 (bottom), MCarter, 22, MO_SES Premium, 16, Solis Images, 18, Steve Byland, 23, SVSimagery, 12, Waldemarus, 10 (speaker); Wikimedia: Axion23, 24, Bri Ham, 25 (top)

All the Internet addresses (URLs) given in this book were valid at the time of going to press. However, due to the dynamic nature of the Internet, some addresses may have changed, or sites may have changed or ceased to exist since publication. While the author and publisher regret any inconvenience this may cause readers, no responsibility for any such changes can be accepted by either the author or the publisher.

CONTENTS

THE NEED FOR SPEED

Superman didn't become the World's Greatest Superhero by waiting for crime to come to him. Wherever super-villains lurk, the Man of Steel taps into his power of speed to track them down. Whether outrunning bullets or flying around the globe, Superman always manages to save the day just in the nick of time.

Superman's speed may be out-of-this-world, but Earth has its own examples of speed that might give the Man of Steel a run for his money. For instance, did you know a hummingbird is considered the world's fastest animal? Or that engineers have developed a rocket car that can break the speed of sound? Want to know more? Take a deep breath and hold on tight. You're about to explore the science behind a world with a need for speed.

FACT:

Superman made his first appearance in *Action Comics* #1 in 1938.

WHAT IS SPEED?

For heroes like Superman, speed is essential to staying one step ahead of criminals. In the scientific world, there's more to speed than getting somewhere in a hurry. But what, exactly, is speed, and how does it affect us every day?

SPEED ESSENTIALS

To scientists, speed is how fast an object is moving. It is a measure of the distance travelled in a certain time. Although speed is often associated with "fastness", any moving object has speed. A tortoise inching along has speed, just not as much as a rocket blasting into space.

While defining speed is simple, perceiving it isn't always straightforward. Superman is famous for travelling faster than a speeding bullet, which is about 2,735 kilometres (1,700 miles) per hour. But right now – even standing still – you are travelling faster.

A person standing near Earth's equator spins about 1,670 kilometres (1,040 miles) per hour around Earth's axis. At the same time, Earth whips around the Sun at 107,800 kilometres (67,000 miles) per hour. That's not all. Our solar system hurtles around the centre of the Milky Way galaxy at about 788,580 kilometres (490,000 miles) per hour. Now that's fast!

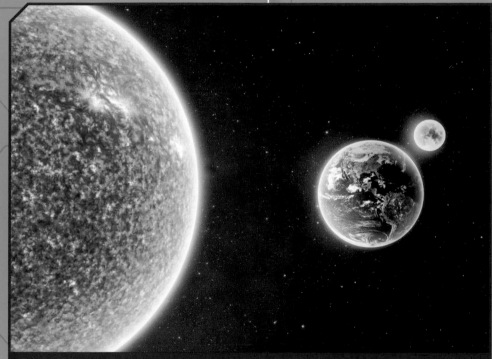

Earth orbits the Sun at the breakneck speed of 107,800 kilometres (67,000 miles) per hour.

STOPPING A BULLET

A speeding bullet only packs a punch when it makes an impact. To stop bullets in the real world, soldiers and police officers use Kevlar. This fabric's strong, tight weave stretches to rob bullets of their energy. Kevlar is the life-saving material used in bulletproof vests.

ACCELERATION

Superman can go from standing still to a blue blur in the blink of an eye. This awesome ability to speed up is called **acceleration**. Acceleration is the change in the **velocity** of a moving object. Imagine travelling in a car on a motorway. As long as the car maintains a constant speed, you don't feel like you are moving. But if the car suddenly speeds up, brakes or turns a corner, you feel it. That's acceleration.

People on rollercoaster feel acceleration as they zoom down a hill.

One of the best places to feel acceleration at work is an amusement park. The thrill of rollercoasters is in their rapid accelerations. The stomach-dropping feeling you get when a rollercoaster plummets down a hill comes from acceleration. As you rapidly speed up, you feel the acceleration. When you squash your friend while rounding a curve, you feel acceleration because your body changes direction. Even the sudden stop at the end of the ride is a form of acceleration called deceleration.

THE WORLD'S FASTEST ROLLERCOASTER

Ferrari World in the United Arab Emirates is home to the world's fastest rollercoaster. Formula Rossa maxes out at 240 kilometres (149 miles) per hour. This speedy coaster accelerates from zero to 100 kilometres (62 miles) per hour in just two seconds.

acceleration rate of change of the velocity of a moving object

velocity measurement of both the speed and direction an object is moving

ULTIMATE SPEED

In the superhero world, you'd do well to round out your track team with Superman and The Flash. Between the two, no one is faster. In our world, you'd definitely want sound and light on your team. Check out the amazing speeds of these two forms of energy.

SPEED OF SOUND

Sometimes Superman flies so fast he becomes supersonic! Supersonic means faster than the speed of sound. Sound is a wave of **vibrations** that pass through air **particles**. Starting at a source, vibrations pass from particle to particle until they reach your ear. These vibrations move through the air at the incredible speed of 1,225 kilometres (761 miles) per hour. That's like running the length of almost four football pitches in one second.

While sound travels fast, its speed is not beyond human reach. Travelling at or beyond the speed of sound is measured in Mach numbers. A vehicle that reaches Mach 1 is travelling at the speed of sound. At Mach 2, it travels twice the speed of sound. At Mach 3, three times, and so on.

The Bell X-1 was the first aircraft to break the speed of sound. On 14 October 1947, Bell X-1 launched from the bomb bay of a Boeing B-29. It then used a rocket engine to go supersonic. Today, most military fighter jets reach speeds of Mach 2 to Mach 3.

Bell X-1

FACT:

On 15 October 1997, the rocket car Thrust SSC became the first car to break the speed of sound. It topped 1,228 kilometres (763 miles) per hour.

vibration fast movement back and forth

particle tiny piece of something

SONIC BOOMS

One big drawback to supersonic flight is the sonic boom caused when jets pass the speed of sound. A sonic boom is a loud rumble caused when air **molecules** are rapidly pushed aside. It is heard and felt by people on the ground when a supersonic plane flies overhead. It can be loud enough to damage people's eardrums and break windows. As a result, supersonic flight is banned over many countries.

An F-18 Super Hornet creates a vapour cone as it nears the speed of sound.

an artist's impression of NASA's X-43A hypersonic jet in flight

While engineers study ways to reduce sonic booms, the race is on to develop **hypersonic** planes that fly even faster. To be called hypersonic, an aircraft must reach Mach 5. On 16 November 2004, NASA's X-43A hypersonic jet set the world record as the fastest aircraft. The unmanned aircraft clocked a speed of nearly 11,265 kilometres (7,000 miles) per hour. That's Mach 9.6!

BOOM!

SUPERSONIC PERSON

Can a human reach supersonic speeds without an aircraft? Felix Baumgartner did it. He jumped from 39 kilometres (24 miles) above New Mexico, USA, on 14 October 2012. On his way down he broke the sound barrier, causing a sonic boom. His maximum speed was 1,340 kilometres (834 miles) per hour.

molecule atoms making up the smallest unit of a substance
hypersonic speed greater than Mach 5

SPEED OF LIGHT

If the speed of sound is incredible, the speed of light is mind-blowing. Light travels at 300,000 kilometres (186,000 miles) per second. At this speed it could circle Earth's equator seven and a half times in just one second.

In fact, the speed of light is so fast we use it to measure huge distances in space. One light year is the distance a light beam can travel in one year. How far is that? About 9 trillion kilometres (6 trillion miles)! If you think the Moon and Sun are really far away, think again. The Moon is only about 1.3 light seconds from Earth. The Sun is about 8.3 light minutes away.

1.3 LIGHT SECONDS AWAY

8.3 LIGHT MINUTES AWAY

Light travels from the Sun to Earth in about 8 minutes and 19 seconds.

The next nearest star to Earth, Proxima Centuri, is 4.24 light years away. When we see Proxima Centuri, we don't see it as it looks now. We see it as it looked more than four years ago. High-powered telescopes, such as the Hubble Space Telescope, help us see stars millions of light years away. But Hubble actually looks back in time. It sees stars as they looked millions of years ago. Some may have burned out before we even discover them.

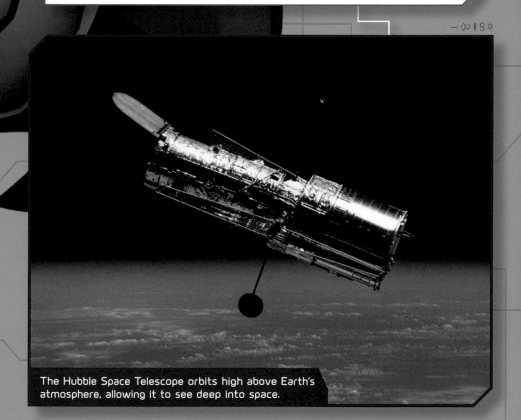

The Hubble Space Telescope orbits high above Earth's atmosphere, allowing it to see deep into space.

JUNO SPACECRAFT

No human invention has come close to achieving light speed. But NASA's Juno spacecraft, launched in 2011, will soon become the fastest human invention. When it orbits Jupiter in 2016 its speed will be about 74 kilometres (46 miles) per second. That's fast, but still just 1/4,000th of the speed of light.

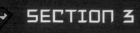
ENEMIES OF SPEED

Just as Superman battles the super-villains of Metropolis, speed has some enemies of its own to overcome. Gravity and friction slow things down.

GRAVITY

What goes up, including Superman, must come down. Gravity is the force that pulls everything towards Earth. You see gravity in action when you throw a ball. No matter how high or fast you throw, eventually the ball returns to the ground.

If gravity's pull is so strong, how do planes and rockets overcome it? An aeroplane's wings create **lift** to fight gravity. The shape and angle of the wing deflects air downwards, creating a push that lifts the plane upwards. The faster an aeroplane travels, the more lift it creates.

Rockets create **thrust** to combat gravity. To break away from Earth's atmosphere a rocket must attain a thrust of 40,230 kilometres (25,000 miles) per hour. Massive amounts of burning fuel spew gases that push off Earth to thrust the rocket into space.

An Atlas V rocket uses the downward thrust of gases to launch towards space.

MICROGRAVITY

As the International Space Station circles Earth, it's constantly falling towards the planet. So why doesn't it hit the ground? Because its speed of 28,000 kilometres (17,500 miles) per hour matches Earth's curve. Inside the station, astronauts feel very little gravity because they are in constant free fall.

lift upward force that causes an object to rise in the air

thrust force that pushes a vehicle forwards

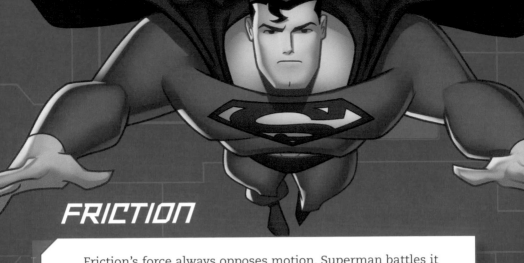

FRICTION

Friction's force always opposes motion. Superman battles it to travel fast. But he also needs it to walk or climb stairs. Friction happens whenever two things rub against each other. Rough surfaces cause more friction, smooth surfaces less. You can keep your balance walking across carpet. Walking on ice is trickier because there is less friction.

Professional athletes can't afford to let friction slow them down. Swimmers wear swimming caps to reduce **drag** from their hair. Many also shave their bodies to limit friction with water. Cyclists shave their legs to fight friction caused by air resistance. Smooth legs help shave time off cyclists' races.

Competitive swimmers wear caps and shave their arms and legs to reduce friction in the water.

Slicks give Formula One race cars extra grip on the road.

While athletes try to reduce friction, race car drivers crave it. Racers use tyres called racing slicks. These tyres may be smooth, but they create more friction than tyres with treads. Since more of the tyre touches the track, its grip is greater. The extra friction steals some speed from the car. But the slick's grip holds the car to the road on tight corners.

HOT BRAKES

Brakes on cars and aeroplanes use friction to reduce speed. This friction generates heat. Aeroplane brakes can reach temperatures of more than 1,000 degrees Celsius (1,800 degrees Fahrenheit). They must be cooled down before they can be used again.

drag force that resists the motion of an object moving through the air or water

SPEED IN NATURE

Superman isn't the only being on Earth with the ability to reach incredible speeds. When it comes to the animal kingdom, he has some competition.

RAPID LAND ANIMALS

If Superman is looking for a competitor in a foot race, a cheetah might be up for the challenge. Cheetahs are Earth's fastest land animals. A cheetah can accelerate from 0 to 97 kilometres (60 miles) per hour in just three seconds. With its amazing speed, it knocks down its prey before attempting a kill.

cheetah

FACT:

The sloth is the world's slowest animal with a top speed of 0.24 kilometres (0.15 mile) per hour. It's so slow that algae grows on its fur.

The cheetah would win a foot race against any animal on Earth, including humans. But speed in the animal world isn't just about how quickly creatures move their legs. In fact, some speedsters have no legs at all. Australia's death adder is one of the fastest striking snakes in the world. It strikes, injects venom and returns to strike position in under 0.15 seconds. Without **antivenin**, 60 per cent of its strikes to humans are deadly.

death adder

antivenin medicine that helps the body to fight off the effects of animal venom

FAST FLIERS

When Metropolis' citizens see Superman in flight, they sometimes mistake him for a bird. It's no wonder. Birds are fast fliers. In fact, the peregrine falcon is the fastest flier in the animal kingdom. When swooping to catch its prey, it travels up to 322 kilometres (200 miles) per hour.

Next to the peregrine falcon, the diving speed of the Anna's hummingbird seems slow. It only reaches speeds of up to 97 kilometres (60 miles) per hour during its dives. But this tiny flier actually moves 385 body lengths in one second, which makes it the fastest animal on Earth. By comparison, the peregrine falcon only moves 200 body lengths per second.

peregrine falcon

Anna's hummingbird

Even more amazing are the **g-force** stunts the Anna's hummingbird performs. G-force is the force felt by a body due to gravity. Standing still we feel 1g – or gravity's normal pull. But on a speeding rollercoaster, we feel greater g-forces when we're pushed against our seats. In fact, the world's fastest rollercoaster produces 1.7g's. And astronauts blasting into space often feel g-forces up to 8g's. But pulling up from a dive, the Anna's hummingbird experiences 10g's!

FACT:

Mosquitoes aren't fast fliers, but they have speedy wings. They beat their wings 500 times per second.

g-force   force of gravity on a moving object

HUMAN SPEED

Nature does its best to rival Superman's power of speed. But humans are drawn to that power too. Whether sprinting on foot or zipping around in high-tech machines, people are always looking for the fastest way to get from here to there.

AMAZING AUTOMOBILES

Superman doesn't need a car to speed him from place to place. But humans are always testing how fast they can travel on four wheels. These days, the fastest cars that can legally take to the roads are called supercars. The current supercar champion is the Hennessey Venom GT. On 14 February 2014, it accelerated from zero to 322 kilometres (200 miles) per hour in just 20.3 seconds. At 435 kilometres (270 miles) per hour, it edged out the Bugatti Veyron Super Sport's previous record by just 3 kilometres (2 miles) per hour.

Hennessey Venom GT

While supercars command the roads, jet dragsters rule off-road. Jet powered dragsters are the fastest cars on Earth. One of the earliest jet dragsters was the Green Monster. It used a J-79 jet engine and axles from a 1947 Ford and a 1937 Lincoln. The Green Monster set three land speed records between 1964 and 1965. Its best speed was 928 kilometres (577 miles) per hour set on 7 November 1965.

the Green Monster on display at an airport near Bournemouth, UK, in 1968

WORLD'S FASTEST HUMAN

Jamaica's Usain Bolt is considered the fastest human in the world. The track star has broken the men's 100-metre world record three times. His fastest time, 9.58 seconds set in 2009, remains unbroken today. At top running speed, Bolt flies down the track at nearly 45 kilometres (28 miles) per hour.

EXTRAORDINARY AIRCRAFT

Land speed records are impressive. But when humans really want to crank up the speed, they mimic Superman by taking to the skies. In fact, the SR-71 Blackbird has a lot in common with the Man of Steel. It's sleek, powerful and can outrun a bullet. The SR-71's speed record of 3,529 kilometres (2,193 miles) per hour, set back in 1976, remains unbroken by any manned jet aircraft. During its 24-year career with the US Air Force, no SR-71 was ever shot down. It flew so high and so fast that enemy missiles never threatened it.

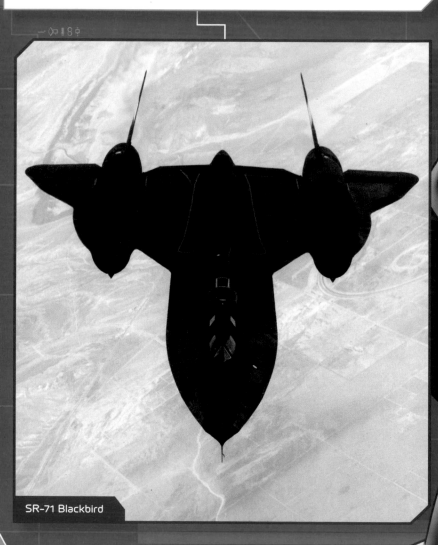

SR-71 Blackbird

North American X-15

Although not a jet plane, the experimental rocket aircraft, North American X-15, actually clocked a speed more than two times faster than the SR-71. At 7,270 kilometres (4,520 miles) per hour, it holds the title as the fastest manned rocket plane. The X-15 was launched from the wing of a B-52 bomber. Each of its flights lasted only about 10 minutes. But they provided engineers with valuable information about aircraft performance at high altitudes and hypersonic speeds. X-15's successes laid the foundation for future space flight.

FACT:

Air resistance made the SR-71's cockpit windows so hot that pilots held their meals to the glass to cook them.

SPEEDY SPACECRAFT

The fastest inventions are those headed out of this world. Escaping Earth's atmosphere and travelling to the ends of the solar system requires maximum speed. To break away from Earth, a spacecraft must travel 40,000 kilometres (25,000 miles) per hour. This speed is called escape velocity.

Usually spacecraft speed is measured relative to the Sun instead of Earth. NASA's *New Horizons* holds the title of the spacecraft with the fastest launch speed. It launched in 2006 with a velocity of 161,000 kilometres (100,000 miles) per hour. In 2015, it reached Pluto and continued onwards to explore a region known as the Kuiper Belt.

an artist's impression of the *New Horizons* spacecraft's encounter with Pluto

The *Helios I* and *II* solar probes hold the title of the fastest objects engineered by humans. Launched in 1974 and 1976, these probes entered orbits around the Sun. The Sun's mass caused them to reach orbital speeds of more than 241,000 kilometres (150,000 miles) per hour.

The *Helios* probes will not hold their title much longer. NASA's *Juno* spacecraft is expected to reach speeds of more than 257,500 kilometres (160,000 miles) per hour in 2016. In 2018, a new NASA spacecraft, *Solar Probe Plus*, will be launched. Its orbital speeds around the Sun will be 724,200 kilometres (450,000 miles) per hour.

Engineers work on the *Helios II* solar probe prior to launch in the 1970s.

 CONCLUSION

Almost nothing slows down the Man of Steel. He can outrun bullets and outfly aircraft. And while his abilities are beyond our grasp, they still remind us that speed affects our lives every single day. From rollercoasters and fighter jets to rocket cars and spacecraft, the science of speed is all around us.

GLOSSARY

acceleration rate of change of the velocity of a moving object

antivenin medicine that helps the body to fight off the effects of animal venom

drag force that resists the motion of an object moving through the air or water

g-force force of gravity on a moving object

hypersonic speed greater than Mach 5

lift upward force that causes an object to rise in the air

molecule atoms making up the smallest unit of a substance

particle tiny piece of something

thrust force that pushes a vehicle forwards

velocity measurement of both the speed and direction an object is moving

vibration fast movement back and forth

READ MORE

Cheetahs (Living in the Wild), Charlotte Guillain
(Raintree, 2015)

Fighter Aircraft (Ultimate Military Machines), Tim Cooke
(Wayland, 2015)

Forces and Motion (Mind Webs), Anna Claybourne
(Wayland, 2014)

Forces and Motion (Super Science), Rob Colson
 (Franklin Watts, 2013)

WEBSITES

www.dkfindout.com/uk/animals-and-nature/cats/cheetah
Cheetahs are super speedy. Find out more on this website.

**www.dkfindout.com/uk/science/forces-and-motion/
understanding-motion**
This website has more information about motion and speed.

INDEX